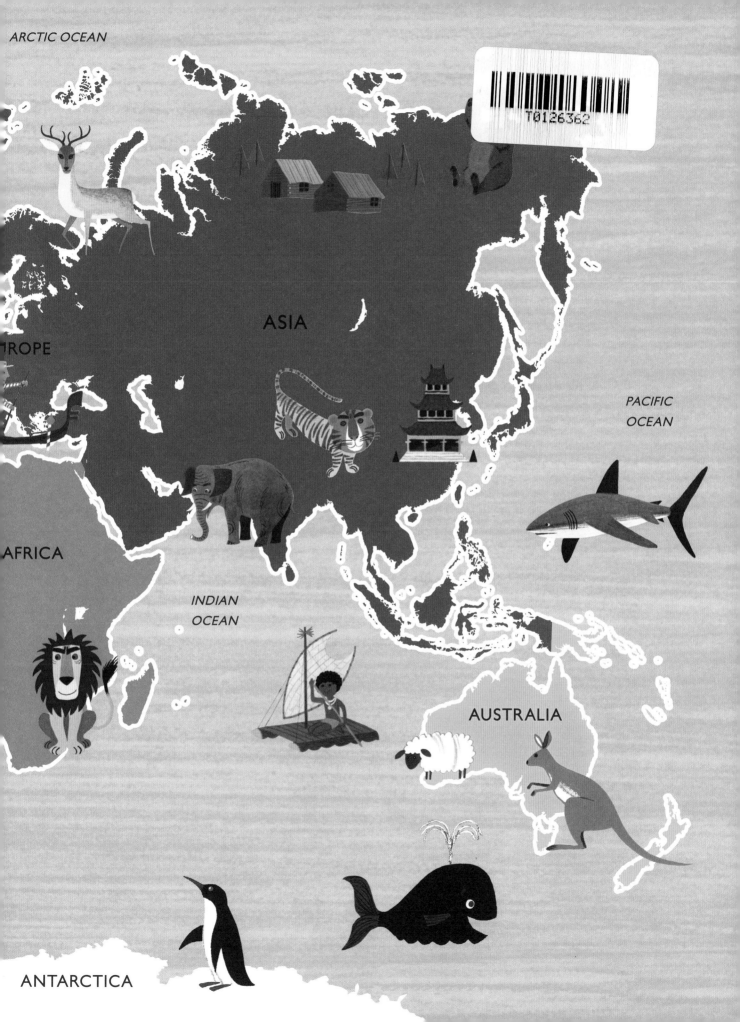

MY ILLUSTRATED
Encyclopedia

MY ILLUSTRATED
Encyclopedia

ALAIN GRÉE

Button
BOOKS

Contents

Flowers

tulip

iris

dahlia

forget-me-not

pansy

anemone

6

poppy

daisy

cornflower

lupin

daffodil

marigold

rose

7

Trees

Did You Know?
A tree has one growth ring for every year it has been alive.

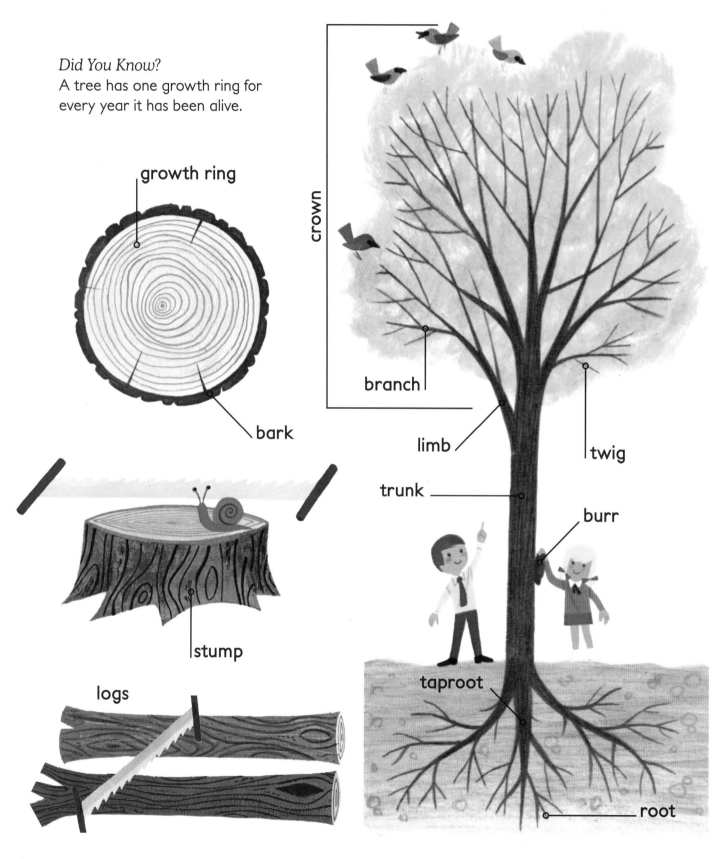

growth ring

bark

crown

branch

limb

twig

trunk

burr

stump

taproot

logs

root

8

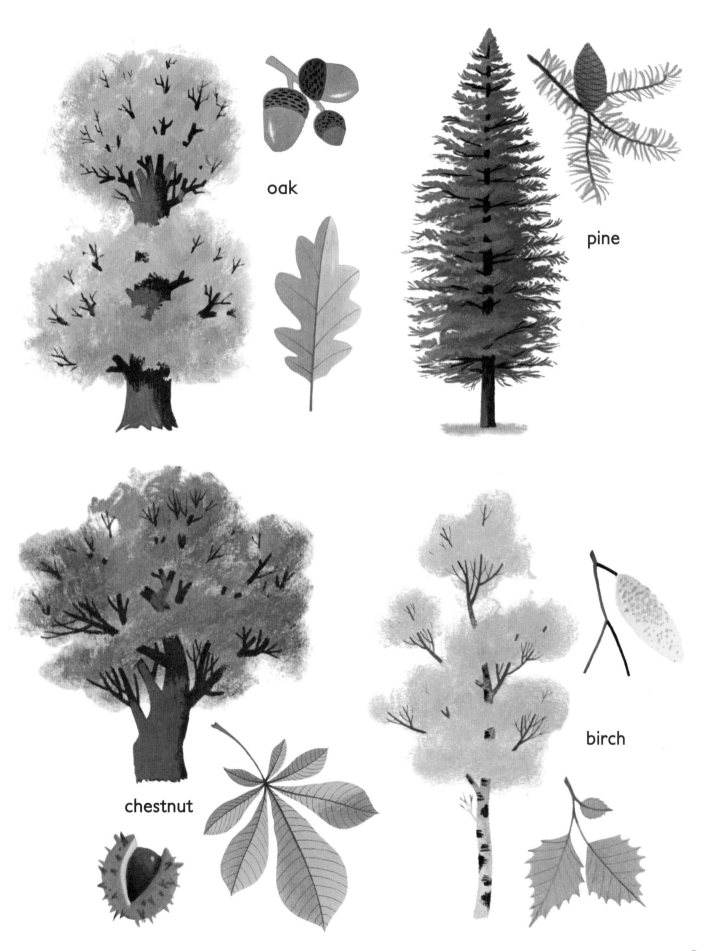

oak

pine

chestnut

birch

9

In the forest

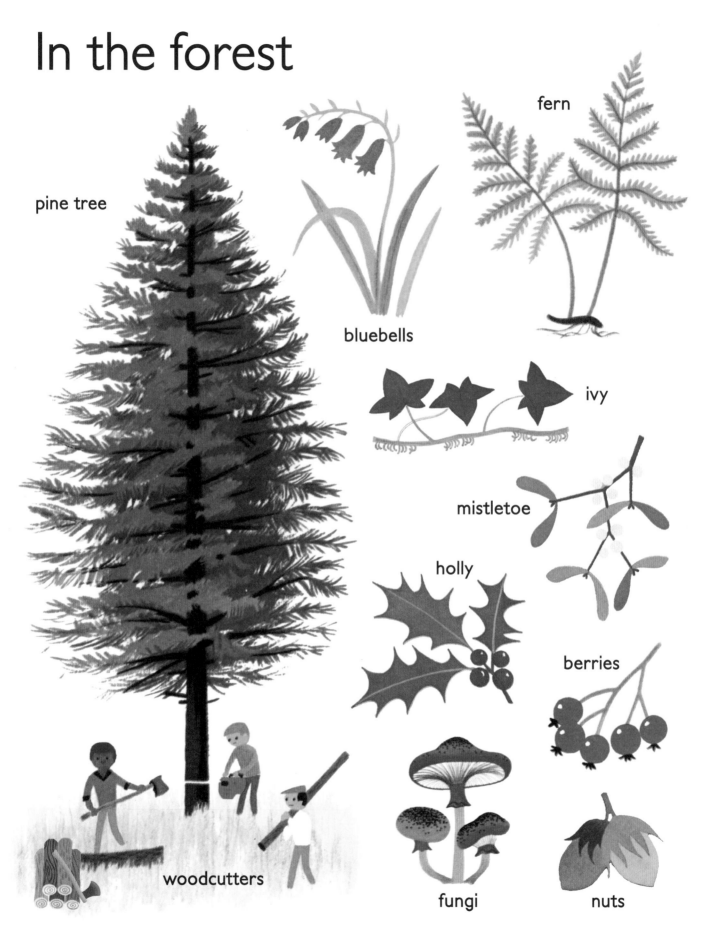

pine tree

bluebells

fern

ivy

mistletoe

holly

berries

woodcutters

fungi

nuts

fox

rabbit

squirrel

pheasant

deer

woodpecker

11

Insects

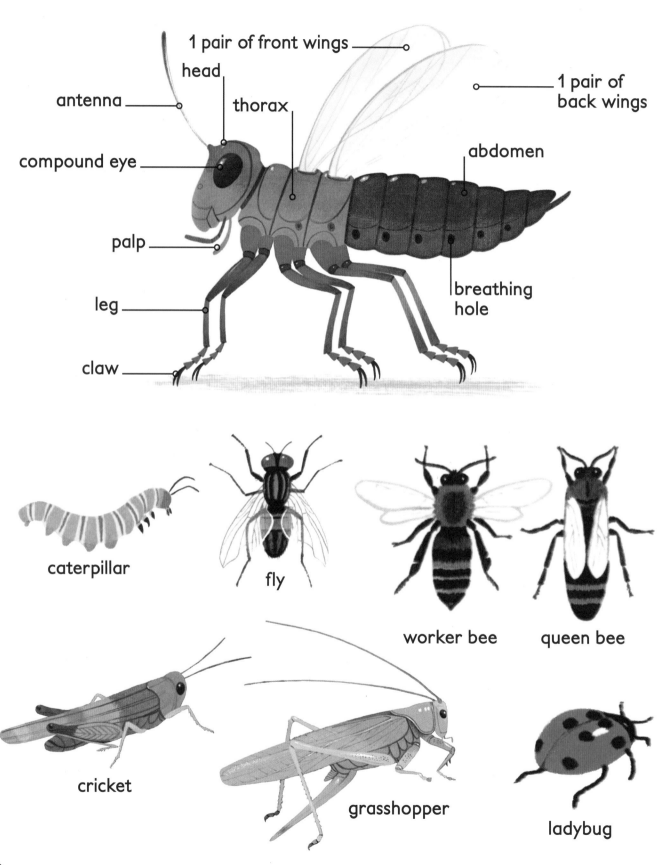

1 pair of front wings

head

antenna

thorax

1 pair of back wings

compound eye

abdomen

palp

breathing hole

leg

claw

caterpillar

fly

worker bee

queen bee

cricket

grasshopper

ladybug

Inside an ants' nest
1. entrances
2. food storage chambers
3. soldier ant protecting the ants' nest
4. worker ant bringing food into the nest
5. worker ants digging a new chamber
6. queen ant laying eggs in her chamber
7. worker ants tending eggs
8. nursery chamber for eggs
9. chamber for larvae (young ants)
10. worker ant tending cocoons

Did You Know?
A queen ant can live for up to 30 years.

ant

Insect camouflage (opposite)
1 This moth larva looks like a branch.
2 The leaf insect mimics the leaves around it.
3 The praying mantis and **4** stick insect both resemble the twigs they hide among.
5 With its wings closed, an underwing moth can rest unseen against a tree trunk.
6 The orange oakleaf or dead leaf butterfly is hard to spot among the real dead leaves.

butterfly

moth

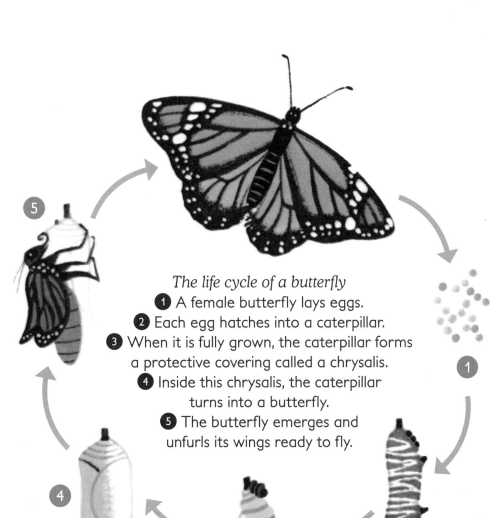

The life cycle of a butterfly
1 A female butterfly lays eggs.
2 Each egg hatches into a caterpillar.
3 When it is fully grown, the caterpillar forms a protective covering called a chrysalis.
4 Inside this chrysalis, the caterpillar turns into a butterfly.
5 The butterfly emerges and unfurls its wings ready to fly.

Did You Know?
Most butterflies fly during the day, whereas most moths prefer to fly at night.

15

Birds

cardinal

jay

sparrow

warbler

wagtail

bullfinch

robin

magpie

lark

swallow

owl

cuckoo

blue tit

crow

toucan

turtledove

pigeon

17

Animal skills and survival

lion

Lions live in packs and work together to hunt for food and protect their young.

emperor penguin

snail

Like the tortoise, a snail uses its armor-like outer shell as a refuge from predators.

tortoise

Many animals like the tortoise hibernate through winter to conserve their energy.

Four layers of feathers and stores of fat keep the emperor penguin warm. It is the only animal that is able to breed during the winter in Antarctica.

The giraffe is the tallest animal in the world. Its long neck and tongue help it to reach food that other animals can't.

A zebra's stripes discourage biting flies by disturbing their vision. No two zebras have the same pattern.

giraffe

zebra

Ostriches can outrun many other animals. Even if a predator does catch up with one, an ostrich will use its powerful kicks to protect itself.

ostrich

gibbon

It may not have a tail, but the gibbon's extra-long arms let it swing through trees at speed, finding food and escaping predators.

goose

Flocks of geese migrate together to spend their winter months in warmer countries.

flamingo

The flamingo uses its long legs to wade through water looking for food, which it then scoops up by bending its long, flexible neck.

Female kangaroos have pouches where they can carry and protect their babies.

kangaroo

hedgehog

elephant

The elephant's trunk is a multi-tool used for breathing, smelling, sucking up water, picking up objects, and cuddling its babies.

Outer spines protect the hedgehog from would-be attackers.

19

frog

toad

otter

River wildlife

swan

goose

heron

stork

kingfisher

dragonfly

great crested
grebe

duck

The seasons

spring

summer

fall

winter

23

The weather

sunshine

rain

lightning

wind

snow

1

2

3

4

fog

Cloud types
1 cumulus (light, fluffy-looking clouds)
2 stratus (flat blankets of cloud)
3 cirrus (high, wispy clouds, like tufts of hair)
4 cumulonimbus (tall, stormy clouds)

Water

clouds

rain

snow

sea

river

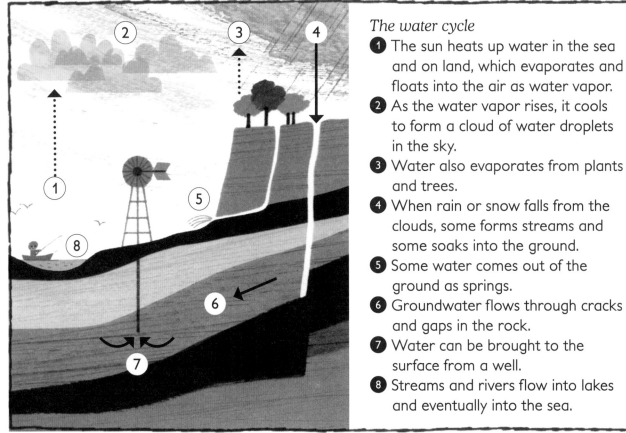

The water cycle

❶ The sun heats up water in the sea and on land, which evaporates and floats into the air as water vapor.

❷ As the water vapor rises, it cools to form a cloud of water droplets in the sky.

❸ Water also evaporates from plants and trees.

❹ When rain or snow falls from the clouds, some forms streams and some soaks into the ground.

❺ Some water comes out of the ground as springs.

❻ Groundwater flows through cracks and gaps in the rock.

❼ Water can be brought to the surface from a well.

❽ Streams and rivers flow into lakes and eventually into the sea.

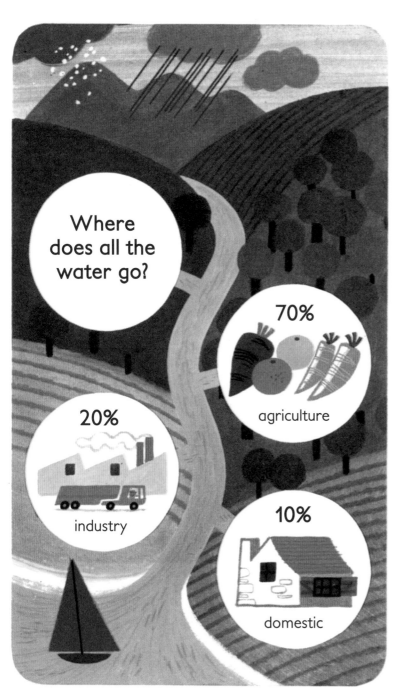

Where does all the water go?

70%
agriculture

20%
industry

10%
domestic

growing plants

feeding farm animals

washing and toilet flushing

cooking

drinking

Did You Know?
People, plants, and animals all need water to live. In fact, we have lots of water stored inside the tiny building blocks (cells) that make up our bodies.

Mountains

Did You Know?
Everest, the world's highest mountain peak, is 29,029 feet (8,848 meters) above sea level.

Mountain flowers
1 soapwort
2 crocus
3 edelweiss
4 aster
5 gentian

A mountain landscape (left)
1. snowline
2. ridge
3. gorge
4. plateau
5. waterfall
6. cliff
7. mountain pass
8. peak
9. lake

cable car

mouflon

chamois

golden eagle

brown bear

29

Rivers

1 source
2 tributary stream
3 river
4 confluence (where two rivers meet)
5 right bank
6 left bank
7 island
8 bridge
9 meander (bend)
10 canal
11 river mouth
12 sea

Did You Know?
The world's longest river is the Nile, which is over 4,000 miles (6,500 kilometers) long and flows through Africa.

30

Freshwater fish

1 eel
2 gudgeon
3 trout
4 perch

5 carp
6 minnow
7 pike

Did You Know?
Salmon are born in freshwater but spend part of their life in the sea. They return to the river to lay their eggs.

salmon

33

Sea life

tuna

octopus

herring

mackerel

plaice

red mullet

skate

34

Did You Know?
Sharks have a really good sense of smell, which helps them to find their prey deep under the water where it is dark.

cod

shark

jellyfish

lobster

swordfish

crab

cockle   cowrie   conch   winkle

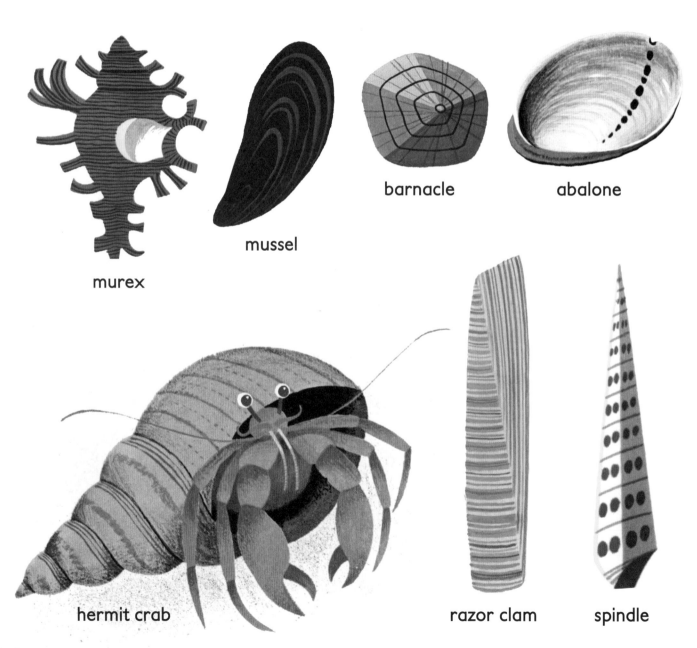

murex

mussel

barnacle   abalone

hermit crab   razor clam   spindle

Under the sea
1. starfish
2. shrimp
3. seaweed
4. sea sponge
5. sponge coral
6. sea urchin
7. sea anemone
8. red soft coral

Did You Know?
A starfish can lose an arm if it needs to, in order to escape an attacker. The arm will eventually grow back.

Farming

sheep

pig

rooster

turkey

hen

chick

38

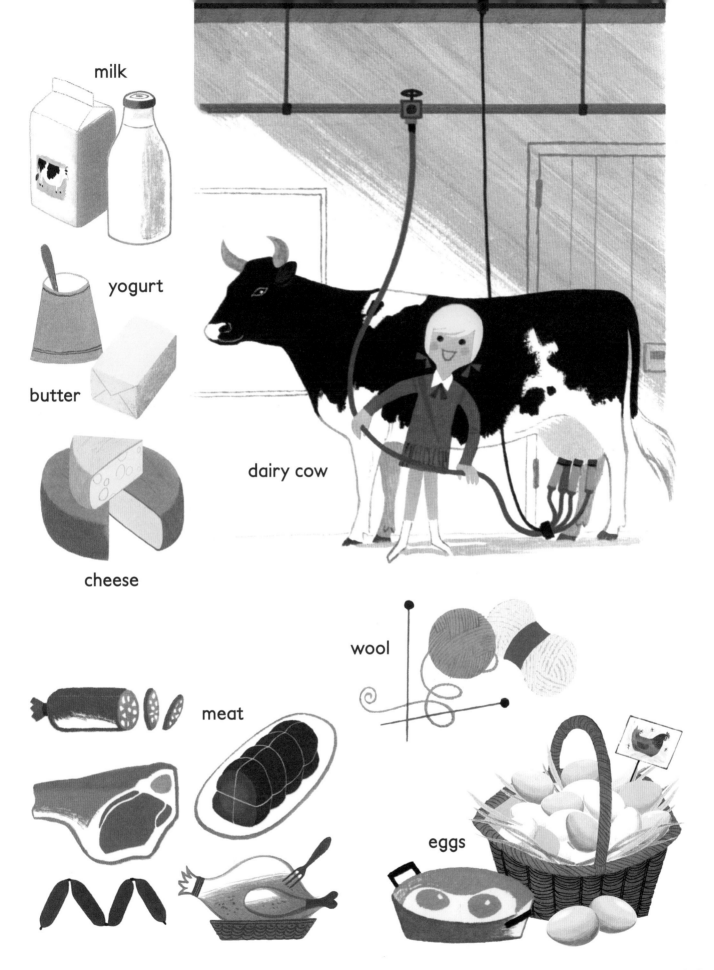

milk

yogurt

butter

cheese

dairy cow

wool

meat

eggs

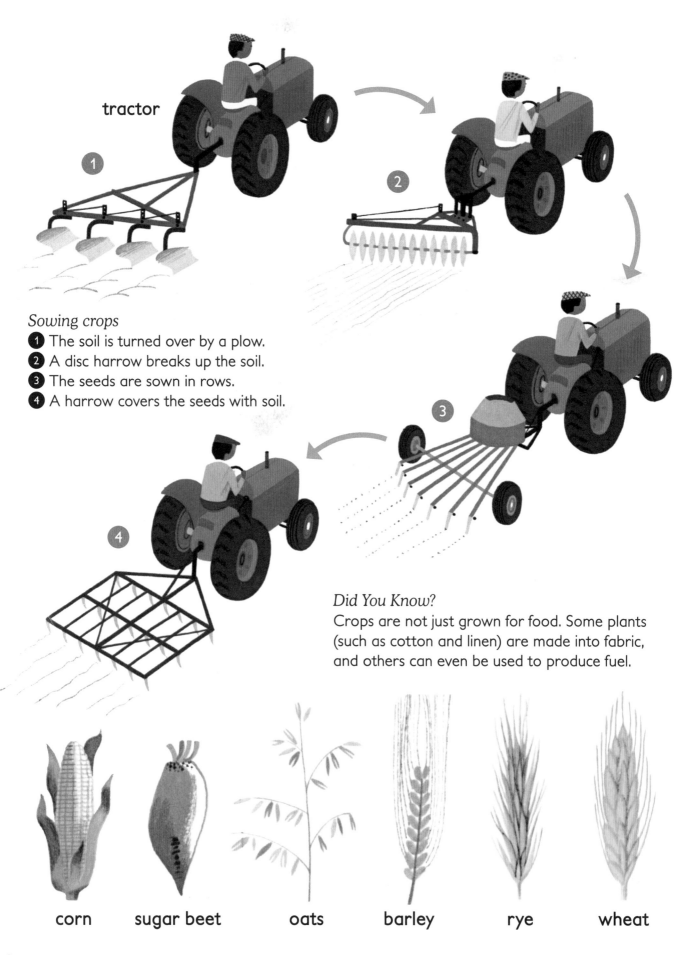

tractor

Sowing crops
1 The soil is turned over by a plow.
2 A disc harrow breaks up the soil.
3 The seeds are sown in rows.
4 A harrow covers the seeds with soil.

Did You Know?
Crops are not just grown for food. Some plants (such as cotton and linen) are made into fabric, and others can even be used to produce fuel.

corn   sugar beet   oats   barley   rye   wheat

combine harvester

From field to loaf

① Wheat is cut by a combine harvester.
② The cut wheat goes into the combine harvester where…
③ …the grains are separated from the stalks.

④ The grains are ground to make flour.
⑤ At a bakery the flour is made into loaves of bread as well as cakes, cookies, pies, and other delicious things to eat.

breakfast cereal   vegetable oil   pasta

animal feed

biofuel

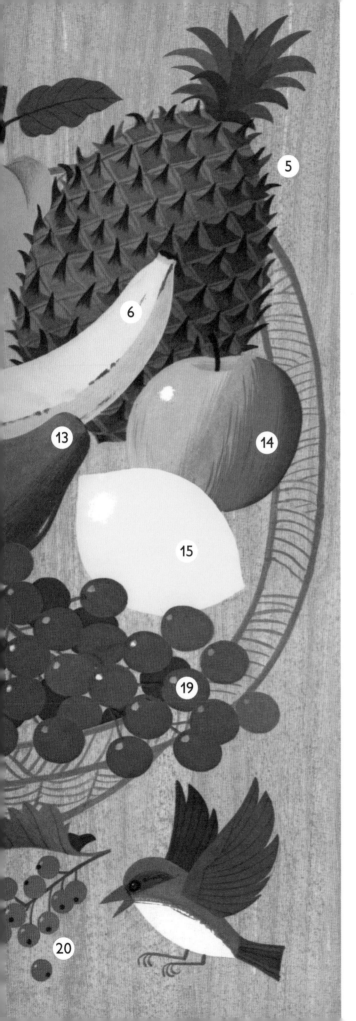

Fruit

1. grapefruit
2. dates
3. raspberries
4. apricots
5. pineapple
6. banana
7. plum
8. peach
9. pear
10. fig
11. pomegranate
12. orange
13. avocado
14. apple
15. lemon
16. watermelon
17. white grapes
18. quince
19. black grapes
20. red currants
21. cherries
22. strawberries
23. mangoes

Did You Know?
A fruit is a part of a plant that contains seeds (or pips). New plants, which will eventually produce more fruit, grow from the seeds. The average strawberry has about 200 seeds.

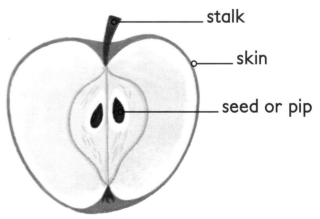

stalk

skin

seed or pip

Vegetables

1. lettuce
2. lentils
3. asparagus
4. eggplant
5. zucchini
6. globe artichoke
7. corn
8. carrots
9. potatoes
10. celery
11. peas
12. tomatoes
13. parsnip
14. cauliflower
15. chicory
16. pumpkin
17. cucumber
18. turnip
19. bell peppers
20. leeks
21. salsify
22. mushrooms
23. marrow
24. scallions
25. shallot
26. garlic
27. spinach
28. green beans
29. beet
30. radishes
31. onions
32. yam
33. sweet potato
34. cabbage

Did You Know?
Many of the foods we think of as vegetables, such as tomatoes, pumpkins, and cucumbers, are fruit because they have seeds.

The garden

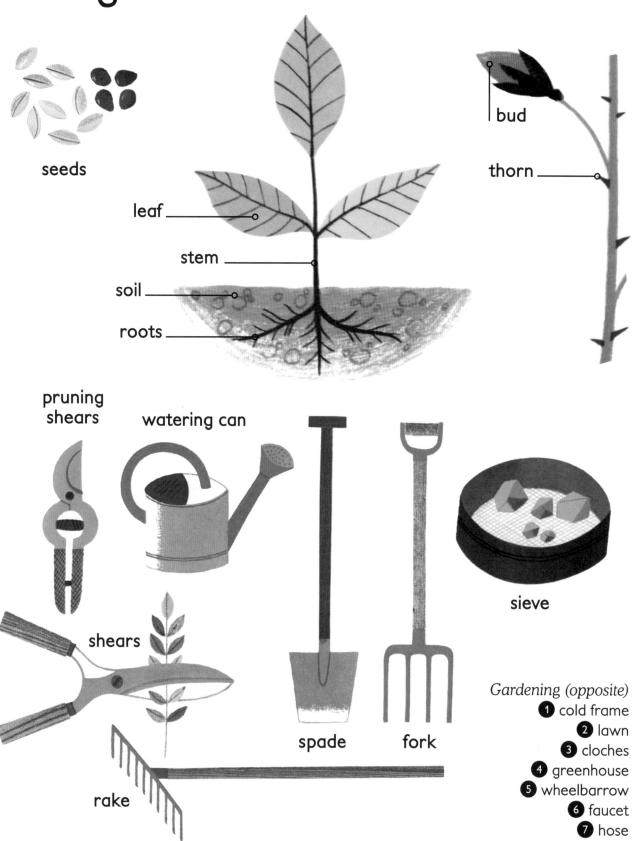

seeds

bud

thorn

leaf

stem

soil

roots

pruning shears

watering can

shears

spade

fork

sieve

rake

Gardening (opposite)
1 cold frame
2 lawn
3 cloches
4 greenhouse
5 wheelbarrow
6 faucet
7 hose

The home

1. roof
2. bathroom
3. bath tub
4. washbasin
5. bedroom
6. closet
7. bed
8. reading lamp
9. attic
10. dining room
11. table
12. shelves
13. kitchen
14. clock
15. stove
16. couch
17. sitting room
18. television
19. light
20. bookshelves
21. armchair

49

Sports

table tennis

soccer

hockey

tennis

rowing

hurdling

rugby

skiing

ice hockey

running

gymnastics

cycling

51

Roads

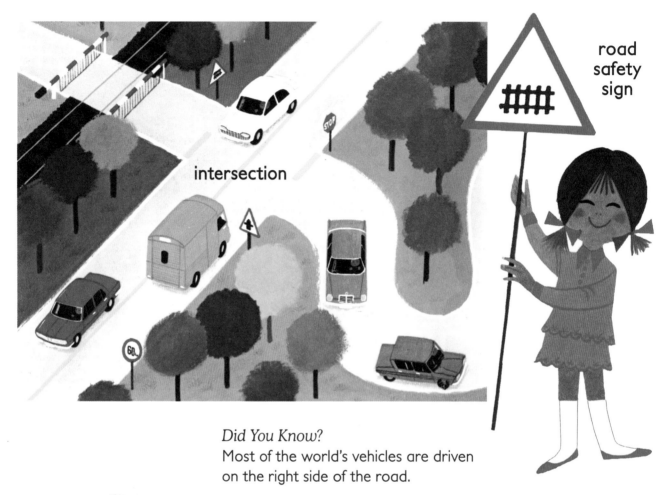

intersection

road safety sign

Did You Know?
Most of the world's vehicles are driven on the right side of the road.

traffic lights

stop   wait   go

safety helmet

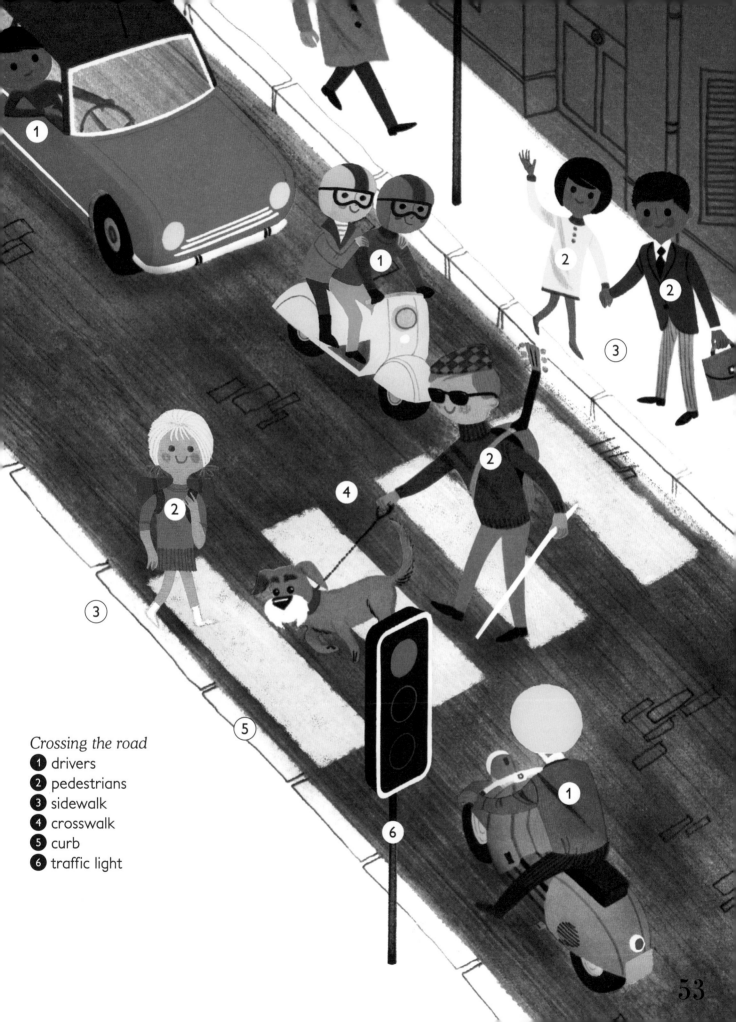

Crossing the road
1 drivers
2 pedestrians
3 sidewalk
4 crosswalk
5 curb
6 traffic light

53

Vehicles

bicycle

moped

motorbike

tram

bus

truck

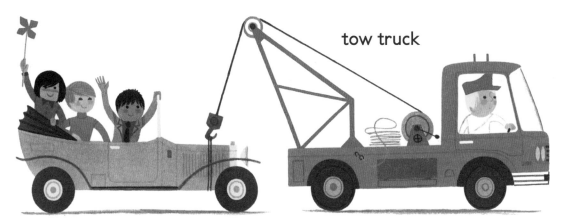

tow truck

tanker truck

fire truck

ambulance

Cars, carts, and carriages

ox-drawn cart in
the Middle Ages

steam-powered carriage (1827)

Parts of a car

1. rear bumper
2. tail light
3. trunk
4. spare tire
5. gas tank
6. rear window
7. back seat
8. seat belt
9. wheel
10. tire
11. driveshaft
12. driving seat
13. steering wheel
14. turn signal lever
15. gear shift
16. accelerator pedal
17. steering column
18. windshield
19. dashboard
20. battery
21. engine

22. fan
23. radiator
24. turn signal light
25. front bumper
26. headlight

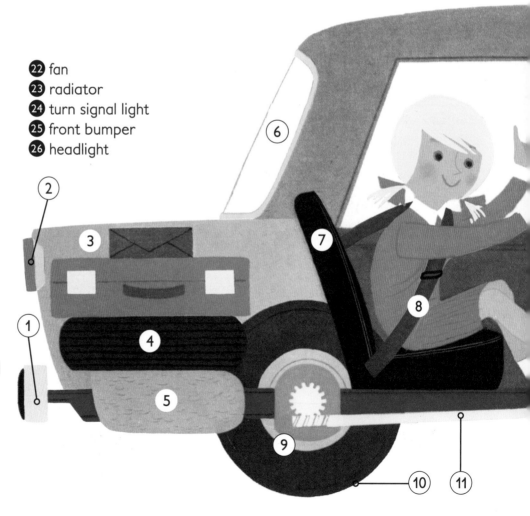

Ford "model T"
(c. 1910)

gas-fueled vehicle (c. 1890)

Did You Know?
Many modern cars are now powered by
electricity instead of a gas-fueled engine.

Railroads

Stephenson's "Rocket"
steam engine (1829)

"DeWitt Clinton" steam
locomotive (1831)

wood-fired steam
locomotive (c. 1850)

electric locomotive

Did You Know?
Some trains have a second locomotive at the back to help push them.

diesel locomotive

freight car

passenger car

59

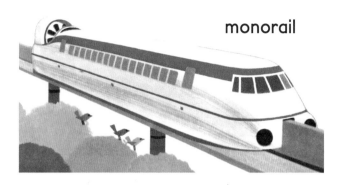

monorail

subway train

funicular
railroad

Crossing mountains and hills
1 viaduct **2** bridge **3** tunnel

60

road traffic waits for a train at a grade crossing

How railroad switches work
Switches allow trains to change tracks.
When the left switch rail is connected **1**,
a train will switch onto the side track.
With the right switch rail connected **2**,
the train will go straight ahead.

switches

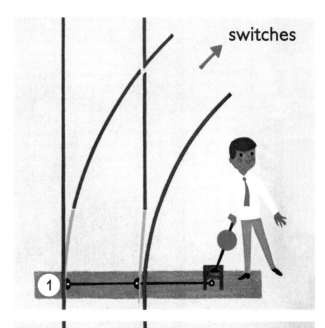

inside a signal tower

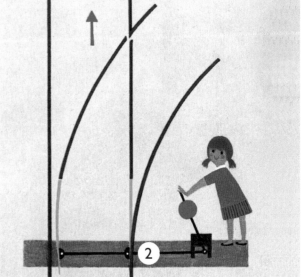

Boats and ships

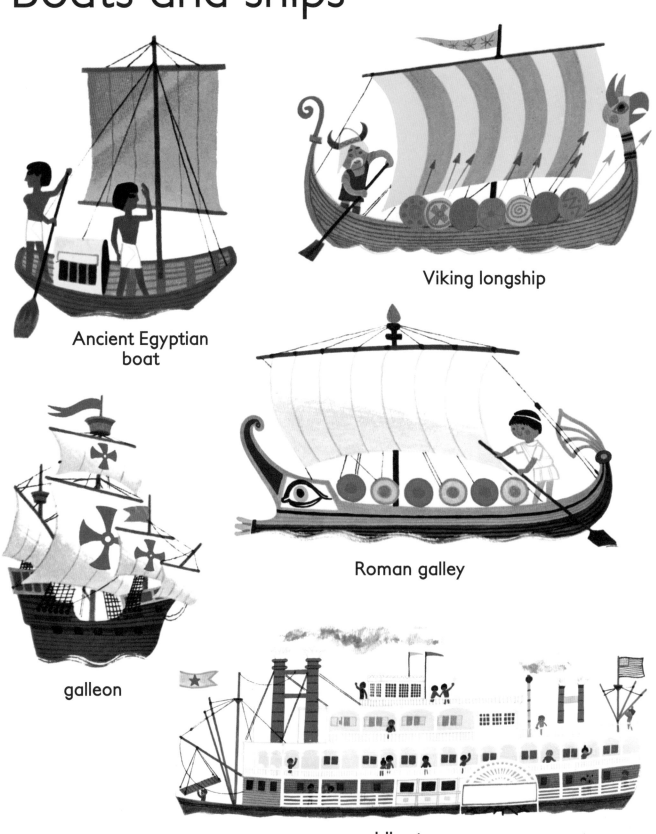

Ancient Egyptian boat

Viking longship

Roman galley

galleon

paddle steamer

canoe

inflatable dinghy

kayak

raft

sailing dinghy

racing yacht

motorboat

63

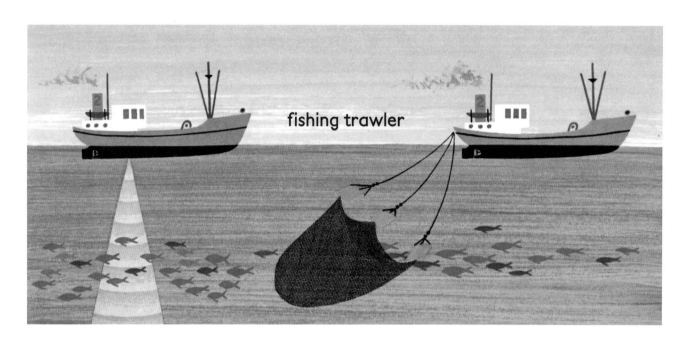

fishing trawler

Did You Know?
A trawl is the name for the net pulled by a trawler boat and used to catch fish.

Inside a trawler
1 pulley
2 storage for nets
3 rudder
4 screw propeller
5 funnel
6 messroom
7 bridge
8 observation deck
9 engine
10 winch (for moving the nets)
11 storage for fish
12 trawl gallows
13 ice tank
14 bunks (beds)
15 fuel tank
16 ventilator
17 anchor

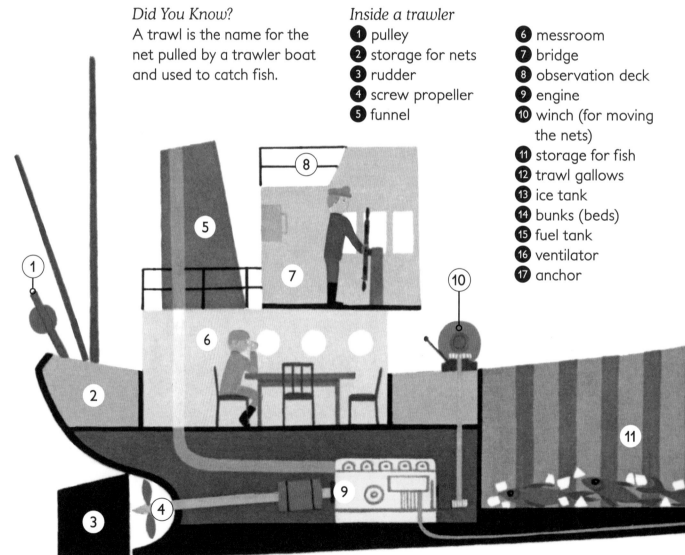

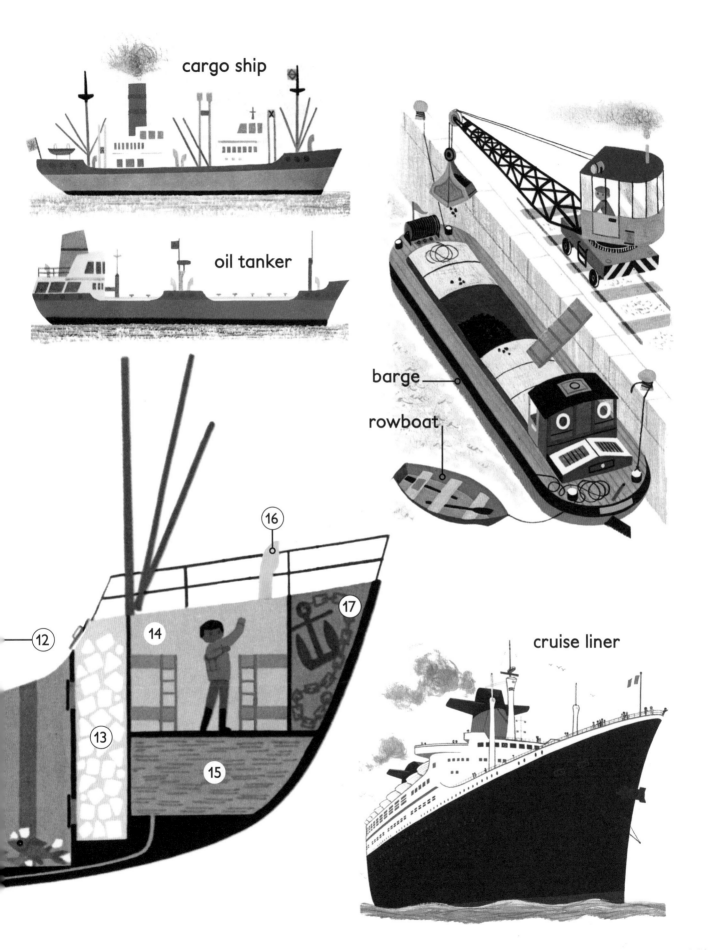

cargo ship

oil tanker

barge

rowboat

16

17

12

14

13

15

cruise liner

Flight

Montgolfiers' balloon (1783)

hang-glider (1896)

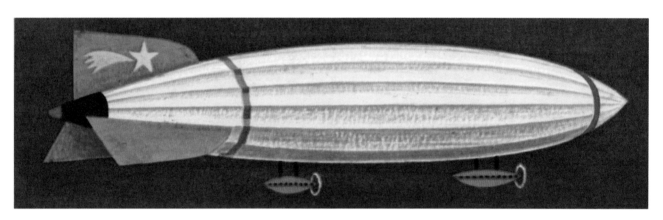

zeppelin hydrogen airship (c. 1900)

biplane (1909)

Louis Blériot crossed the English Channel in 1909.

Did You Know?
A glider is a type of airplane that does not usually have an engine.

glider

parachute

helicopter

seaplane

67

airport

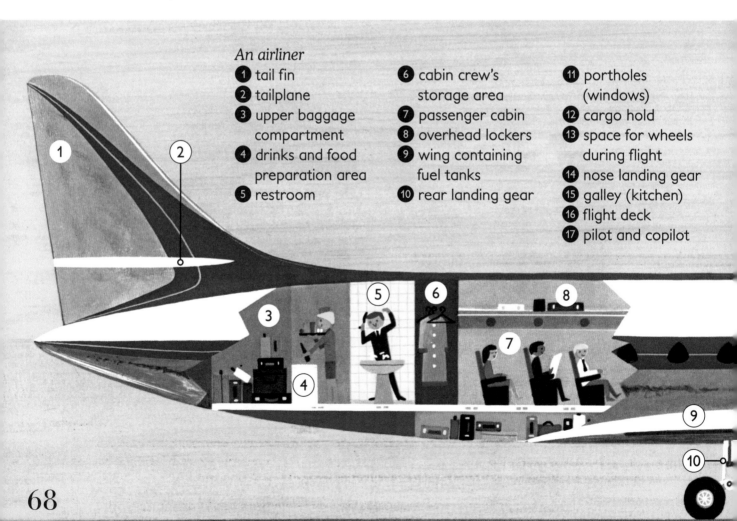

An airliner
1. tail fin
2. tailplane
3. upper baggage compartment
4. drinks and food preparation area
5. restroom
6. cabin crew's storage area
7. passenger cabin
8. overhead lockers
9. wing containing fuel tanks
10. rear landing gear
11. portholes (windows)
12. cargo hold
13. space for wheels during flight
14. nose landing gear
15. galley (kitchen)
16. flight deck
17. pilot and copilot

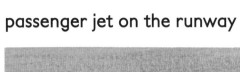

passenger jet on the runway

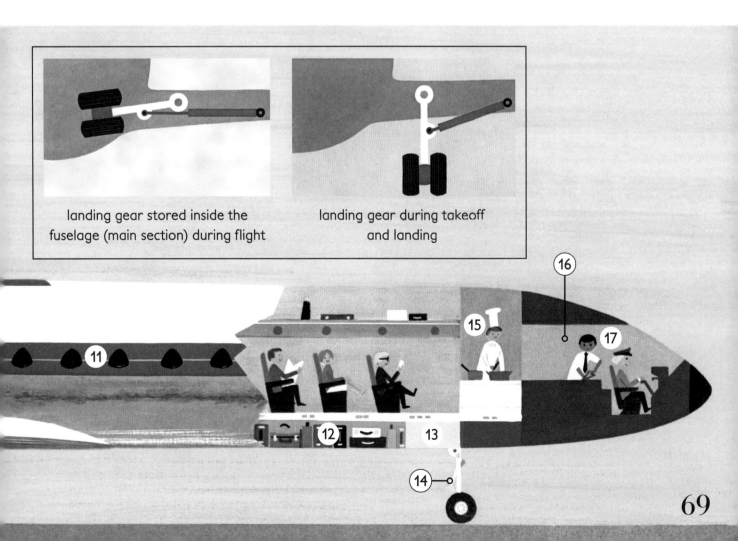

landing gear stored inside the
fuselage (main section) during flight

landing gear during takeoff
and landing

69

Energy

gas

electricity

solar power

oil

wind power

coal

70

hydroelectric power station

Oil and its uses

oil rig

fuel

5813
00024

cooking

heating

refrigeration

detergents

polishes

printing inks

foam
sponges

cosmetics

plastics

paints

tires

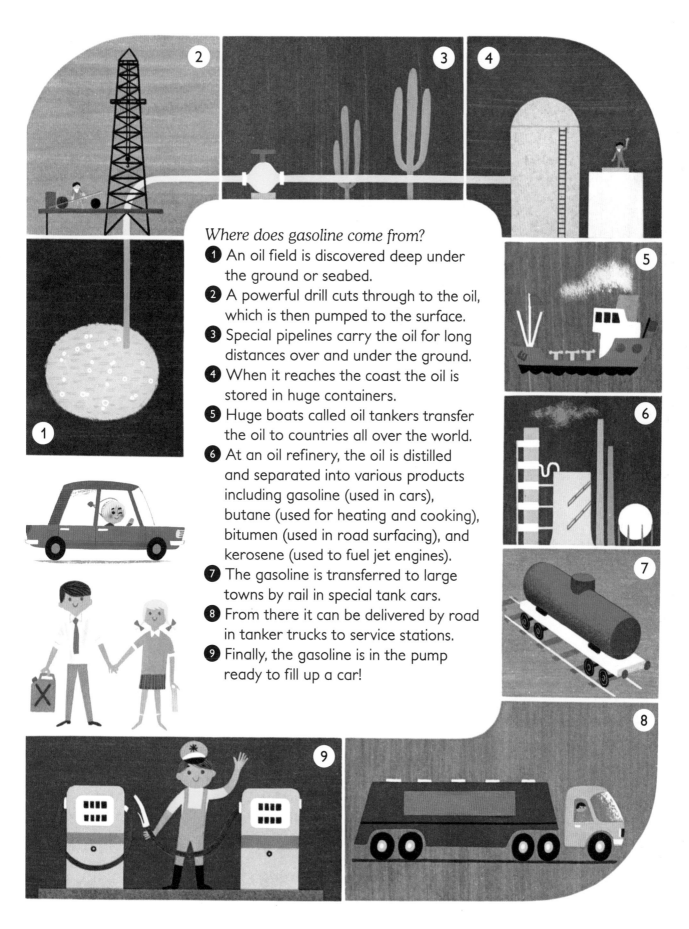

Where does gasoline come from?

1. An oil field is discovered deep under the ground or seabed.
2. A powerful drill cuts through to the oil, which is then pumped to the surface.
3. Special pipelines carry the oil for long distances over and under the ground.
4. When it reaches the coast the oil is stored in huge containers.
5. Huge boats called oil tankers transfer the oil to countries all over the world.
6. At an oil refinery, the oil is distilled and separated into various products including gasoline (used in cars), butane (used for heating and cooking), bitumen (used in road surfacing), and kerosene (used to fuel jet engines).
7. The gasoline is transferred to large towns by rail in special tank cars.
8. From there it can be delivered by road in tanker trucks to service stations.
9. Finally, the gasoline is in the pump ready to fill up a car!

Space

The Solar System
1. Neptune
2. Uranus
3. Saturn
4. Jupiter
5. Mars
6. Earth
7. Venus
8. Mercury
9. Sun

The colored circles (right) show the order the planets appear in and their sizes in relation to each other.

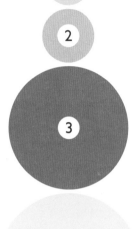

The Sun is over a hundred times larger than the Earth, while the Moon is only about a quarter of its size.

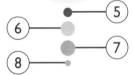

Sun

Earth

Moon

The phases of the Moon

We can see the Moon from Earth because it reflects light from the Sun. The Moon travels around the Earth (shown below), taking about 27 days to complete its journey. As it moves, different amounts of it are hit by the Sun's light, which affects how it appears to us on Earth (shown right), from a New Moon (1) to a Full Moon (5).

how the Moon appears to us from Earth

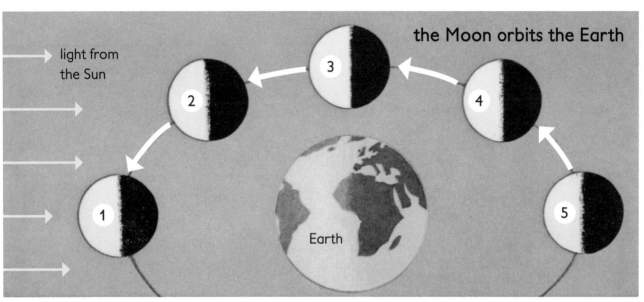

light from the Sun

the Moon orbits the Earth

Earth

The first liquid-fueled rocket was built by Robert H. Goddard (1926).

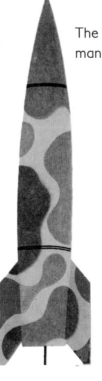

The V2 missile was the first man-made object in space (1942).

A dog called Laika was the first living creature to orbit the Earth (1957).

The first manned mission to land on the Moon was Apollo 11. It was launched into space by a rocket called Saturn V.

Apollo 11 space capsule

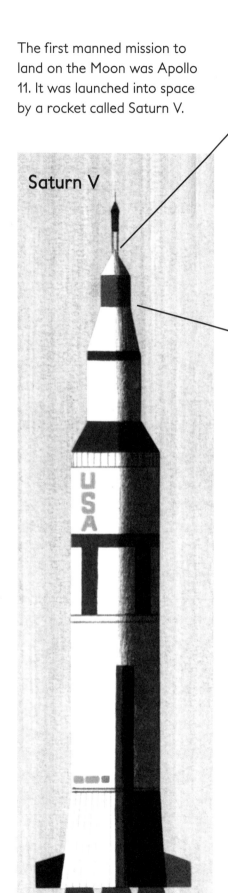

Saturn V

rocket launch

Did You Know?
The first human being to walk on the Moon was Neil Armstrong on July 20, 1969.

moonwalk

Did You Know?
The Moon is moving farther away from the Earth by a tiny bit every year.

Index

For more on Button Books, contact:

GMC Publications Ltd
Castle Place, 166 High Street, Lewes, East Sussex, BN7 1XU
United Kingdom
Tel +44 (0)1273 488005
www.buttonbooks.co.uk

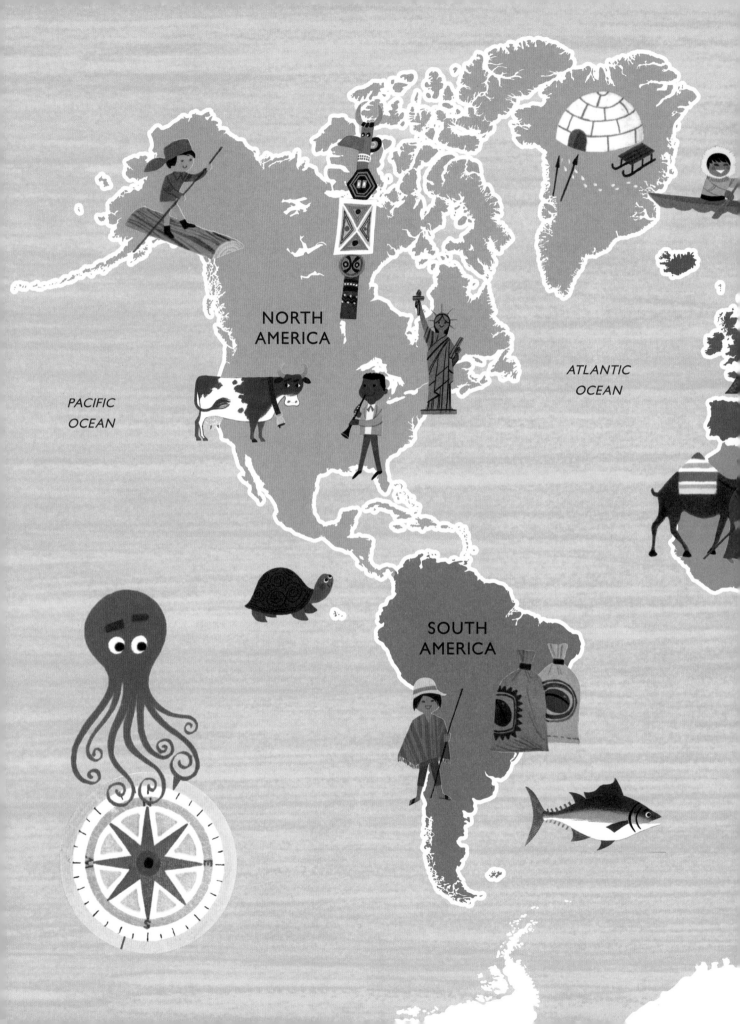

NORTH
AMERICA

PACIFIC
OCEAN

ATLANTIC
OCEAN

SOUTH
AMERICA